SNAP SHOT™

Senior Editor
Mary Ling

Editor
Caroline Bingham

Art Editor
Joanna Pocock

Designers
Sara Hill, Jane Thomas

Production
Catherine Semark

Consultant
Phil Wilkinson

A SNAPSHOT™ BOOK

SNAPSHOT™ is an imprint of Covent Garden Books.
95 Madison Avenue
New York, NY 10016

Photography by Christi Graham, Peter Hayman, Michael Holford, Colin Keates, Nick Nicholls, Harry Taylor, Michael Zabe

2 4 6 8 10 9 7 5 3 1
All rights reserved.

Every effort has been made to trace the copyright holders and we apologize in advance for any unintentional ommissions. We would be pleased to insert the appropriate acknowledgment in any subsequent edition of this publication.

ISBN 1-56458-728-2

Color reproduction by Colourscan
Printed and bound in Belgium by Proost

INCREDIBLE

BURIED TREASURE

Written by
Christopher Maynard

Contents

Ancient Greek
clay jug with coins
found buried
beneath a temple

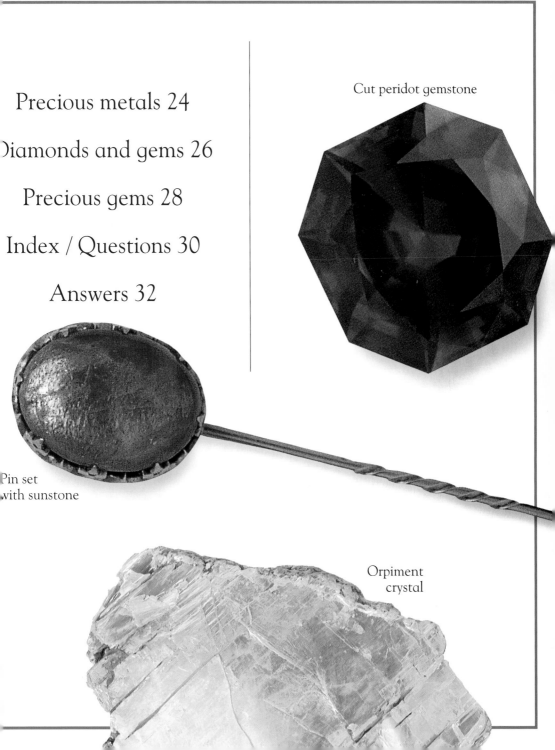

Cut peridot gemstone

Pin set
with sunstone

Orpiment
crystal

Tut's treasure

In November 1922, the English archaeologist Howard Carter found the tomb of the Egyptian king, or pharaoh, Tutankhamen. It had been hidden for 3,200 years!

Mummy case

Tutankhamen was placed in three coffins, one inside the other. The inner one was made of solid gold and contained the preserved body, or mummy, of the king.

Golden shrin

Four golden shrines stoo around the pharaoh coffin. Behind the swinging doors so sacred statue

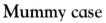

The case of the missing king!

Death mask
The pharaoh's mummy wore a mask of solid gold inlaid with gems. It shows how young Tutankhamen looked when he died. He was probably no older than 20.

*ll Egyptian
ngs wore
striped headdress.*

Where's my mummy?

Not only pharaohs, but most rich Egyptians were mummified after death. Their bodies were meant to last forever.

Decorated with religious symbols

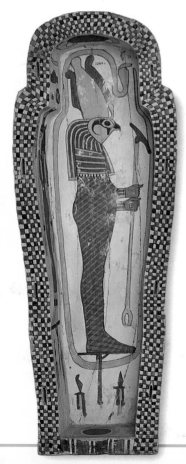

Message boxes
Mummy cases were painted with scenes from the afterworld.

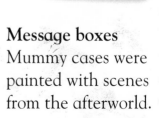

Last supper
Ancient Egyptians believed that the dead could still eat and drink in the afterworld.

Hard at work even after death!

Say "aahh"
After death, these tools were used in a special ceremony called the Opening of the Mouth to help the mummy eat and drink."

To rest for some
Mummies were often buried with models of workers, called *shabtis*, who carried farming tools. Shabtis served their masters after death.

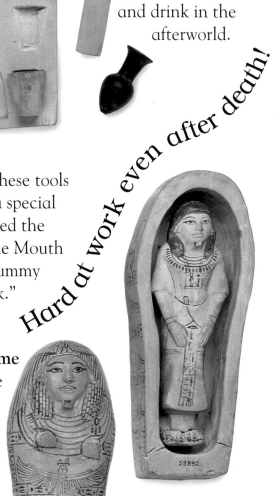

This wooden mummy case was painted gold to make it look much finer.

9

The riches of Greece

We can learn a lot about people who lived in the past through the treasures we find, from fabulous ornaments to everyday things. The objects shown here all date from the time of the ancient Greeks.

Olive oil is a favorite flavoring.

Oil's well in the kitchen
This little dolphin is a container for olive oil. The ancient Greeks were a seafaring people who respected the dolphins that swam around their coasts.

Dolphin oil contain

Whose mask?

This gold mask was found in Mycenae, Greece. It was once thought to be Agamemnon, a Greek king. But the true answer remains a mystery.

This owl is a symbol of Athena, goddess of wisdom.

The face of a 3,600-year-old king?

This coin was found on the isle of Aegina.

Spare change

The Greeks were the first people to use coins. They made them out of gold or silver, and stamped them with symbols of their gods.

Roman treasure

Treasures that belonged to Roman citizens 2,000 years ago can tell us many things, from what people wore to the amount of money that they earned.

Golden wonders
Beautifully crafted jewelry was worn by the rich women of Rome.

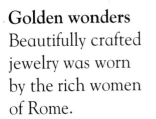

The Roman empire stretched ...

Back pay
This hoard of gold coins was over four years' pay for a Roman soldier. It was buried in England and then forgotten.

These solid gold earrings are shaped like dolphins, a popular form.

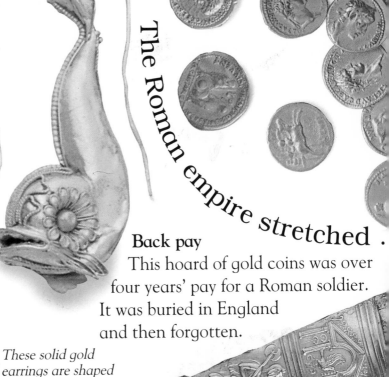

Arm bag

Roman soldiers carried their money in a small leather or metal purse worn on the arm like a bracelet. The lid faced in, so the purse could only be opened when it was taken off.

The head of the emperor and his honorary titles

Lid

cross Europe, Africa, and the Middle East.

Roman sword scabbard

Present swords!

This unusual scabbard was presented to a soldier by a grateful Emperor Tiberius. It is made of wood and richly decorated with gold and silver.

A portrait of Emperor Tiberius

American gold

In the years before Columbus reached the Americas, three great civilizations flourished the areas of Mexico, Central America, and Peru: the Aztec, the Maya, and the Inca.

This figure is the Inca sky or moon god.

People asked their gods for …

Riches of the Incas
When Europeans first met the Incas of Peru, they were stunned by the Incas' wealth of gold, silver, and gems.

Inlaid with turquoise and highly valued by the Incas

The Incas worshiped jewel-covered statues of their gods.

Bowl of blood
This reclining statue holds a bowl for the hearts and blood of people sacrificed to the Aztecs' gods.

Dog bites man
This fierce coyote mask from the early city of Tula was worn by a warrior. It is decorated with mother-of-pearl.

Statue guarded the shrine of "Tlaloc," the god of rain.

...od crops and a healthy life.

Chacmool – a sacrificial statue

15

Funny money

Money doesn't have to be made out of gold or silver to be valuable. After all, today we use paper or plastic to buy things. But teeth, shells, and stones have also been used as money!

For some peoples, perforated stones, teeth, and

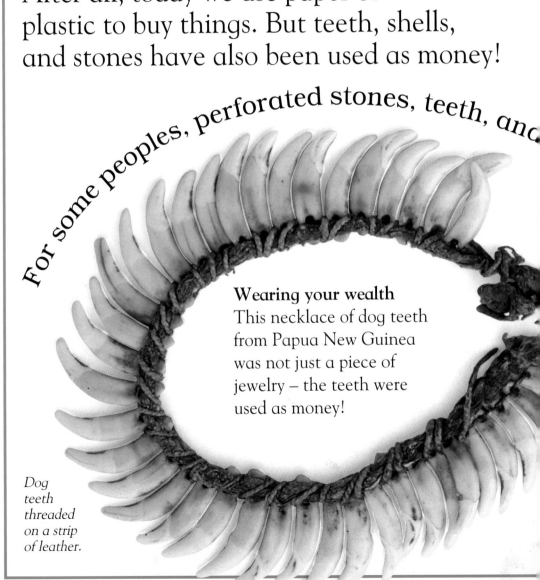

Wearing your wealth
This necklace of dog teeth from Papua New Guinea was not just a piece of jewelry – the teeth were used as money!

Dog teeth threaded on a strip of leather.

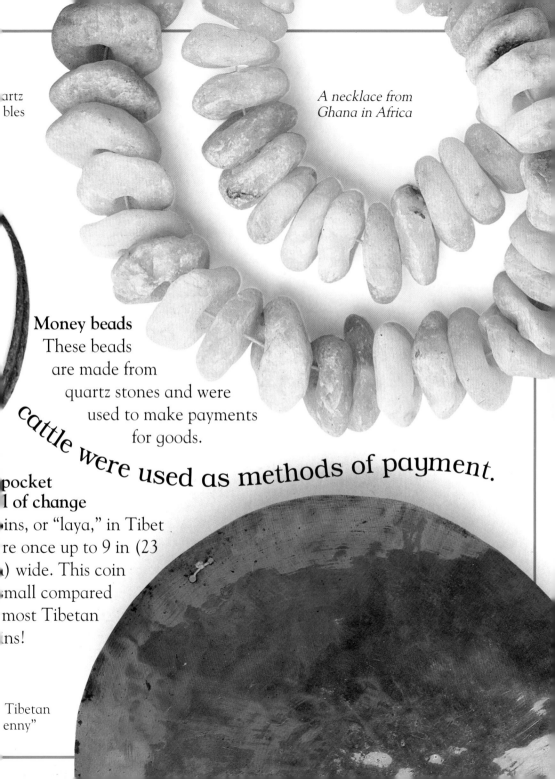

artz
bles

*A necklace from
Ghana in Africa*

Money beads
These beads
are made from
quartz stones and were
used to make payments
for goods.

cattle were used as methods of payment.

pocket
l of change
ins, or "laya," in Tibet
re once up to 9 in (23
) wide. This coin
mall compared
most Tibetan
ns!

Tibetan
enny"

Precious stones

The stones you kick around as you walk aren't valuable. But some stones, such as turquoise, agate, lapis, and jade, are rare and beautiful. They are used to make jewelry and precious ornaments.

Digging for lapis
The best lapis of all comes from Afghanistan, where it is mined from quarries of white marble.

Beautiful, brilliant, and blue, too

Lapis is easy to polish into beads for making necklaces.

The name lapis comes from the Persian word "lazhward," which means "blue."

A gem called lapis
Lapis lazuli was used to decorat masks thousands of years ago in Babylon and Egypt. Its brilliant blue color comes from small amounts of sulphur in the stone

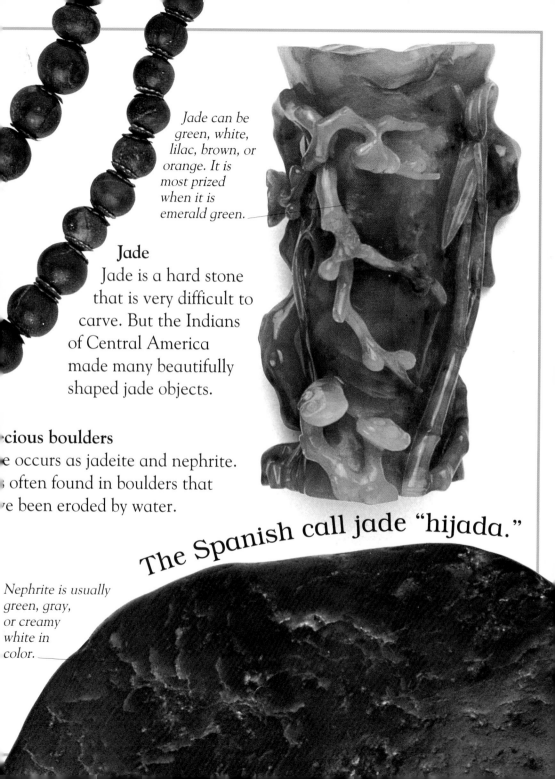

Jade can be green, white, lilac, brown, or orange. It is most prized when it is emerald green.

Jade

Jade is a hard stone that is very difficult to carve. But the Indians of Central America made many beautifully shaped jade objects.

·cious boulders

e occurs as jadeite and nephrite.

; often found in boulders that

·e been eroded by water.

The Spanish call jade "hijada."

Nephrite is usually green, gray, or creamy white in color.

Trapped in time

Nature keeps its own history. Animals die and become fossilized in rock. Insects fall to a sticky end, trapped in amber forever.

A glass coffin
Millions of years ago, insects became stuck in oozing gum. Today they remain perfectly preserved inside chunks of hardened gum, called amber.

This insect is preserved in amber.

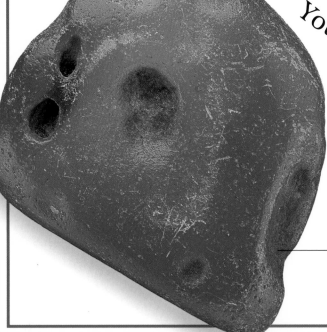

You can find fossils ...

Rocky resin
Amber looks and feels like a rock, but it is really the fossilized gum of coniferous trees.

Its glassy, yellow-brown color makes amber good for jewelry.

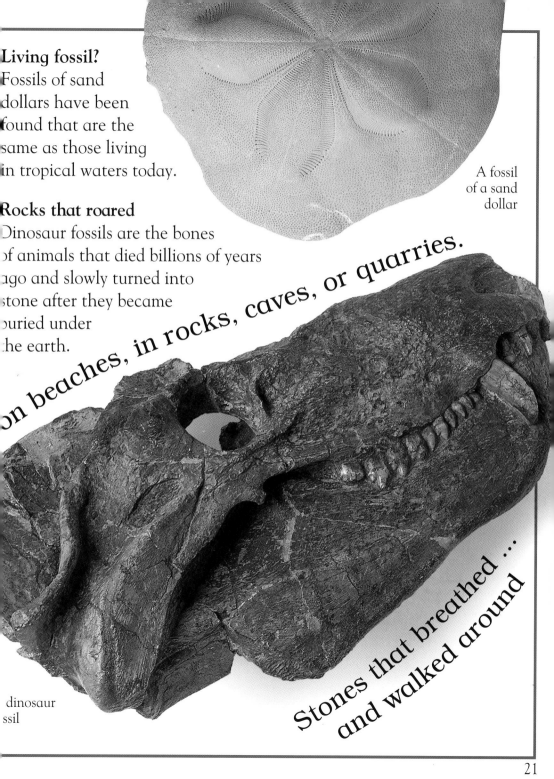

Living fossil?

Fossils of sand dollars have been found that are the same as those living in tropical waters today.

Rocks that roared

Dinosaur fossils are the bones of animals that died billions of years ago and slowly turned into stone after they became buried under the earth.

A fossil of a sand dollar

on beaches, in rocks, caves, or quarries.

Stones that breathed ... and walked around

dinosaur fossil

21

Treasures from the sea

Coral, shells, and pearls are naturally made by ocean animals. Pearl divers in Japan, known as *amas,* hold their breath and dive to depths of nearly 40 ft (12 m) to collect pearl oysters.

Pearly colors
Pearls can be gold, pink, or black in color.

Annoyed oysters
Pearls are made when a grain of sand enters the shell of an oyster or mussel, irritating the animal. The grain is slowly coated with smooth layers of a substance called "nacre", forming a pearl.

Huge pearl oysters are found in the oceans around Australia and Malaysia.

Does a pearl have a mother?

Mother-of-pearl is also made of nacre, just like pearls.

Mother-of-pearl
The shells of animals called "abalones" have smooth, bright blue-green linings made of mother-of-pearl.

Living skeletons under the sea

Red and blue coral is especially prized.

Colorful creatures
Coral is formed from the skeletons of tiny animals that live in colonies in tropical waters. It varies in color from black to cream.

Precious metals

Since the days of the
ancient Egyptians, more
than 5,000 years ago, gold
and silver have been widely
treasured. Today a third metal is
even more valuable – platinum.

Fool's gold

Platinum

Platinum power
This metal has become
extremely valuable because
it is used in oil refining,
and to reduce pollution
from car exhausts.

Any fool's gold
"Fool's gold" is
really iron pyrit
Its bright, brass
color is easy to
mistake for gol

There are over 80

*At the front of
this tiara is a tiny figure
of the god Eros, holding a jug.*

Silver shot
Silver is used in many things, including photography. Today most silver comes from copper and lead-zinc mines.

This lump of silver-flecked ore was found in Kongsberg, a famous silver mine in Norway.

Silver ore

Gold crush
Goldsmiths enjoy working with gold because it is a soft metal and can be easily bent and hammered into shapes.

Alexander the Great captured this treasure when he conquered Persia in 334 BC.

different types of pure metals.

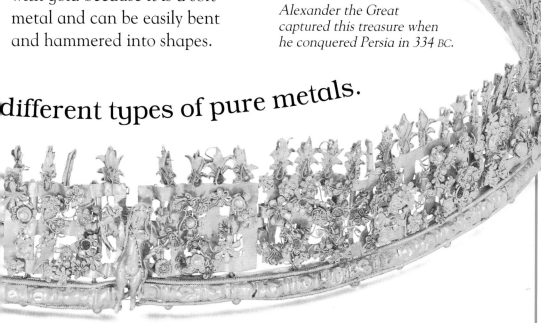

Diamonds and gems

Diamond is the hardest of all known minerals, and the most valued, too. Its name comes from the Greek word *adamas*, which means unconquerable!

Deep diamonds

Diamonds are formed deep within the Earth's crust, under enormous pressure. Most of the world's best diamonds are mined in South Africa.

This gold snuff box, made for Tsar Alexander II of Russia, is studded with 16 big diamonds.

The biggest diamond in the world

King of the stones

This is a replica of the Cullinan diamond. It is the biggest diamond ever found. Discovered in a South African mine, it weighs 3,016 carats.

Ruby love

For a long time, red rubies were symbols of power and romance. They were often given as tokens of love.

Ruby

ems are cut into special shapes.

Amethyst . . . hic!

In the past, some people believed that the purple amethyst stone cured drunkeness.

Amethyst

Some Egyptian emerald mines date back to 1650 BC!

Emerald

Emeralds . . . hiss!

Emeralds are a rich green color and come mainly from South America. They were once thought to blind snakes.

Amethyst

Garnet

Precious gems

There are more than 3,000 kinds of minerals in nature, but only a few are rare, beautiful, and har enough to be cut into gems.

Tourmaline

Tourmaline comes in the widest range of colors of all gems. Its crystal shape leads to different colors even within the same stone. "Watermelon" tourmaline, for example, has a pink core and green outer edges.

All the colors of the rainbow

Zircon

Pure zircon is colorless and looks a lot like diamond. If zircon has a color, it means the gem has impurities.

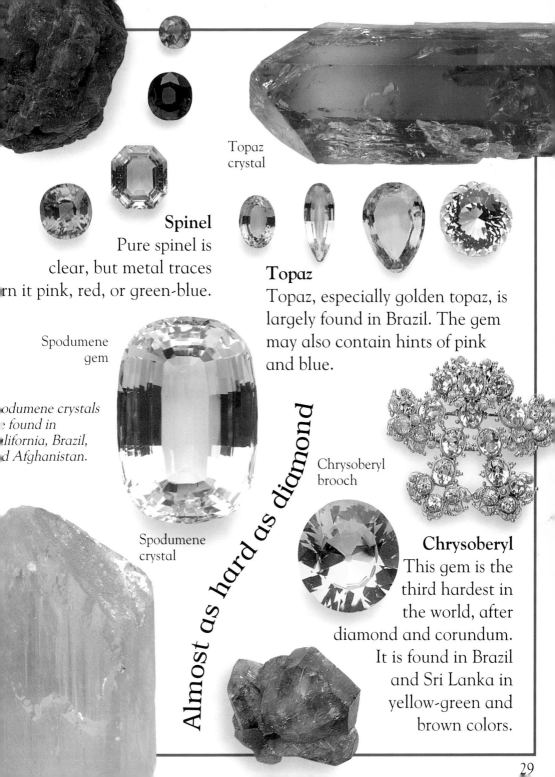

Spinel
Pure spinel is clear, but metal traces rn it pink, red, or green-blue.

Topaz crystal

Topaz
Topaz, especially golden topaz, is largely found in Brazil. The gem may also contain hints of pink and blue.

Spodumene gem

odumene crystals
e found in
lifornia, Brazil,
d Afghanistan.

Chrysoberyl brooch

Spodumene crystal

Almost as hard as diamond

Chrysoberyl
This gem is the third hardest in the world, after diamond and corundum. It is found in Brazil and Sri Lanka in yellow-green and brown colors.

29

Index

Five fiendish question

1. Who was buried in a coffin of solid gold?

2. Which people first used gold and silver coins?

3. Where in the world could you once pay for things with dogs' teeth:
a) Australia?
b) Canada?
c) China?
d) Papua New Guinea?
e) Hawaii?

4) What rare and beautiful treasure is yours if you find a boulder of nephrite?

5) What metal is more valuable than gold?

Answers on page 32

Answers

From page 30:

1. Tutankhamen, an ancient Egyptian pharaoh
2. The ancient Greeks
3. In Papua New Guinea necklaces of dogs' teeth were used as money
4. Nephrite is the mineral from which we get jade
5. Platinum

S/97   IMM4